Welcome to

CREEPERS® Mysteries

I hope you brought a flashlight...

CREEPERS® Mysteries
The series that has everyone *talking...*
from **Movies for the Ear**®

Haunted Cattle Drive
Creepers Mysteries—Book 1
Book & Movie for the Ear Script

Haunted Cattle Drive, The Audio
*Audie Award Winner for Best Original Program
from the Audio Publishers Association*

Toadies
Creepers Mysteries—Book 2
Book & Movie for the Ear Script

Screams at Maybe Mansion
Creepers Mystery Party Game

Visit us at www.creepersmysteries.com

This copy of

CREEPERS® Mysteries
Book 1

Haunted Cattle Drive
belongs to:

Pinkgirl

_____

Your Autograph

idea

—A soul stops
gets out of
A body ← ya

Published by Movies for the Ear,® LLC

Copyright ©2013 ©1996 Connie Kingrey Anderson

Printed in the United States of America.
For information, address Movies for the Ear, LLC, 8362 Tamarack Village, Ste. 119-327, Saint Paul, MN 55125

Cover art ©2010 Movies for the Ear,® LLC

Movies for the Ear® is a registered trademark of Movies for the Ear, LLC.

Library of Congress Cataloging-in-Publication Data
Anderson, Connie Kingrey.
    Haunted Cattle Drive – Creepers Mysteries series – Book 1 / by Connie Kingrey Anderson
    Summary: Harry, Gillian and Arvin visit Smokey Joe's Ranch and go on an authentic cattle drive. They find out just how authentic when they land in the middle of a century-old mystery between a bandit and a bounty hunter from the Old West.

ISBN 978-1-935793-00-7 (paperback)
ISBN 978-1-935793-01-4 (E-book)
ISBN 978-1-935793-02-1 (CD)
    [1.Ghosts – Fiction. 2. Westerns – Fiction. 3. Performing Arts.]
    I. Anderson, Connie Kingrey. II Title. III. Series

Library of Congress Control Number: 2012930438

Visit us at www.creepersmysteries.com

Dedication

For Ebeneezer Stump,
who appears and disappears
at just the right times...

CREEPERS® Mysteries
Haunted Cattle Drive
THE BOOK

Haunted Cattle Drive—The Book
Turn the lights down low, and crank the fun up high!
Read it with a flashlight, if you dare!

CREEPERS® Mysteries

Haunted Cattle Drive

MOVIE FOR THE EAR SCRIPT

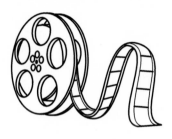

CREEPERS® Mysteries

Haunted Cattle Drive

The Book

By Connie Kingrey Anderson

Cover art by B.J. Nartker

Movies for the Ear®

Chapter 1

Road to Smokey Joe's Ranch

When the sun dips low in the western sky, there's a hazy glow on the bluffs. Some say if you ride too long in the saddle, you start to see things in that glow. Some say you can see the faces of long dead bandits rolling in the tumbleweeds. They skitter into your path, then blow just out of your reach. The same way those old bandits stayed one step ahead of the law, and out of the noose...

Smokey Joe started the tired old engine. He tightened his grip on the steering wheel to keep it from shaking. Carefully, he guided the tourist bus over the bumpy dirt road. When the engine settled into a steady hum, he smiled and looked in the rear view mirror.

"Howdy everybody, I'm Smokey Joe!" His voice boomed like a Hollywood tour guide performing for a packed bus. But there were only three people in it. "Just sit back and enjoy the bus ride out to my ranch. Feast your eyes on cowpoke country." He nodded toward the two red-headed kids sitting behind him. "Now, what did you say your names were?"

"I'm Harry," said the boy. "And this is my sister Gillian."

"Hi," Gillian waved at Smokey Joe's reflection in the mirror.

Smokey Joe tapped his forefinger to the brim of his worn leather cowboy hat. Then he pushed it up slightly, showing a pale forehead above his brown, weathered face.

"I like to check out everybody I haul out to Smokey Joe's Ranch, just to see if they match any pictures on the WANTED POSTERS. Don't want you sliding up to a can of beans at my table, only to find out you're a couple of low down, no good varmints."

Harry leaned forward in his seat and said matter-of-factly, "Our mom's travel agency is going to start booking vacations on your ranch, so we're trying it out for her."

"Hey..." On the other side of the aisle, a dark-haired boy leaned out of his seat, feeling somewhat ignored.

Harry poked his thumb at him. "Oh, and this is Arvin."

"I can introduce myself." He stood up to his full height, then lifted his chin, as if that would add another inch. "I'm Arvin."

Smokey Joe gave him a sideways look. "I thought only two city slickers were coming out here to get prickly burrs in their britches, Marvin."

"That's *Arvin*. And yeah, they're the two city slickers. I'm an experienced horseman." The bus hit a bump in the road, and Arvin fell back into his seat with a hard and humbling smack.

"Arvin thinks he's an expert, but he's only the extra ticket," Gillian said smugly. "Buy two, get one free."

"Gillian, your mom begged me to come along because you don't have a clue."

"We still have to pay tax and destination charges," Gillian said. "Otherwise, Arvin's free."

Chapter 2

The Disappearing Cowboy

"Hey, Harry." Gillian tried to get her brother's attention. He was scrunched down in his bus seat so he couldn't be seen. He peered around the edge of the cracked red upholstery.

"Hellooooo. What are you doing?" She started to knock on his head with her knuckles, like he was a door. But he quickly grabbed her wrist and pushed it away.

"Shhhh. Look," he said.

"At what?"

"There's a cowboy in the back of the bus," he whispered, "and there's something really weird about him."

"What cowboy?" Gillian said, a little too loud.

"Shhh!!" Harry slunk down lower. "In the last seat. He's got a silver hat, silver hair, and silver tooth."

"You're hiding from nobody, Harry. There's no one back there. Turn around."

Harry spun around, then jumped out of his seat. "Hey! He's gone! Where did he go?"

Gillian rolled her eyes. "There's no place to go on a moving bus."

"But, he *was* there," Harry said, spooked. How could he have disappeared into thin air?"

Arvin, who was dozing, spoke without opening his eyes. "Thin air is common in high altitudes, Harry. There's less air getting to your brain."

"You should know airhead," Gillian said.

Chapter 3

The Beadiest Eyes in the West

It was a long, lonely road out to Smokey Joe's Ranch. The wind whistled through the bluffs, and tumbleweeds skittered across the deserted road.

All three kids dozed in their bus seats, using their jackets as pillows. Only Smokey Joe was awake to see the day drift into a cold, pitch black night. He struggled to see the bumpy dirt road in front of him, but it was almost impossible. The crooked bus headlights snaked their way through the darkness, lighting only odd patches here and there.

Suddenly, out of the darkness there was a sound of metal clinking against metal. It started in the distance and gradually moved closer. Harry heard it first and opened one eye. Then he opened both eyes and looked around the bus. It was strange to hear something, but not be able to see it.

He listened just a little longer before he poked his elbow into his sister's side. "Gillian, wake up."

She ignored him, turned over, and punched up the jacket under her head.

"Gillian, listen! Listen to that sound!" He shook her shoulder.

"Wha...wha...what are you talking about?" she reluctantly opened her eyes. But it didn't really matter since everything was dark. "Why did you wake me up, Harry? I'm tired."

"Shhh...listen." They were both quiet and the sound of metal clinking against metal filled the bus.

"What is that?" Gillian whispered, suddenly alert.

"I don't know," he said. "Is it Arvin?"

"She squinted at Arvin who was lying across two seats, snoring like a buzz saw. "No, he's asleep."

Harry looked toward the hazy headlights at the front of the bus. "Maybe it's Smokey Joe..."

"No, he's sitting in one place," Gillian said. "And the sound is moving. It's getting closer."

"You're right. It almost sounds like...like someone tossing coins!"

"But where's it coming from?" Gillian turned toward the sound, then turned again, and again. "It keeps changing direction!"

"I don't know. It's so dark I can't see a thing."

"I don't understand," Gillian said in a low voice. "We're the only ones on this bus."

"Except for that cowboy."

"There's no cowboy, Harry!"

"Well somebody's making that noise," Harry whispered. "And whoever it is..."

"...is getting closer," Gillian said.

The clanking of coins became louder and faster. Suddenly, it was right behind Gillian's head! She jumped out of her seat in a panic. She waved her hands as if batting away flies. "It's around my head! The sound is in my hair! This is creepy, Harry! I'm scared!"

"Aaahh!" Smokey Joe hollered. "Get outta the way!"

The brakes screeched, and Smokey Joe lost control of the bus. It skidded, then landed in a ditch.

"Aaahh!" Gillian screamed. "There's a face in the windshield!"

Harry jumped up—he couldn't believe what he was seeing! "Man alive!"

"No, he's not. Look!" Gillian pointed.

"It's just a face," Harry stared in amazement, "and it's floating!"

It was a Prospector from the old Gold Rush days. He had black hair, a black hat and a big toothless grin. The Prospector laughed an eerie, other-worldly laugh, and chanted, "Dead Man Jack, never look back. Dead Man Jack, never look back." Then he laughed again.

Suddenly, the Cowboy with the Silver Tooth appeared—the one Harry had seen earlier. The Cowboy slowly slithered up from behind the last seat in the bus. He pushed up the brim of his silver hat and squinted at the Prospector.

Then the Cowboy walked down the aisle of the bus, his spurs jingling with every step. He planted his boots squarely in front of the windshield. "Why you no count, good for nothin', silver mining thief... I'll teach you to go prospecting in my saddlebags!"

The Prospector laughed, "You think you can take me, you double-crossing snake? Eyeball to eyeball?"

"Eyeball to eyeball," the Cowboy growled. I'll stare you down if it's the last thing I do." He fixed his eyes on the Prospector and blasted him with an angry stare.

The Prospector let out a cackling laugh. "You forget, I've got the beadiest eyes in the West." The Prospector glared back at the Cowboy with eyes so hot they almost sizzled. The Cowboy became weak and drenched in sweat.

The Cowboy snarled, gasping for air, "I'll get you, you stinkin' Prospector, you low down lizard." The Cowboy struggled to pull a small box of matches from his pocket. He lit one match and held it in front of his shiny silver tooth.

The light ricocheted off the silver tooth and shot toward the windshield. The beam blasted away the Prospector's floating face. "Aaahh!"

When the Cowboy blew out the match, the Prospector was gone.

Harry turned to Gillian. "Did you see that?"

"Wh...What was it?" she stammered.

"I think it was a...a..."

"...a slight delay," Smokey Joe turned over the bus engine. "Just a slight delay. Are you kids alright? I had a sudden turn there. But we'll be on our way again in no time."

"Smokey Joe, who was that in the window?" Harry asked.

"Who? You mean what. A big old tumbleweed was what it was, Harry. Rolled smack across the windshield."

"No, it was a toothless old Prospector," Harry insisted. "He had black hair and a black hat."

"And his face was floating!" Gillian exclaimed.

Smokey Joe shook his head. "Now, you kids are lettin' your imaginations run away with you, like a couple of broncos that ain't been broke yet."

Harry jabbed a finger at the windshield. "That face said 'Dead Man Jack, never look back.'"

"Dead Man Jack?" Smokey Joe thought for a moment. "You must have been dreaming about those WANTED POSTERS over there on the front seat. There it is, right on the top."

Harry picked up the top poster from the pile and examined it. "Hey Gillian, look at this." He read,

"Wanted: Dead Man Jack. Notorious train robber, bank robber and stage coach robber. Bounty hunters welcome. "

Gillian nodded. "That's the guy alright."

Smokey Joe took off his cowboy hat and ran his hand over his ghostly white forehead. "You kids forget that the poster is over 100 years old."

Harry was beginning to understand. "So the guy we saw is..."

"Dead. Dead as a doornail."

Gillian looked at the windshield. "So that floating face was...a ghost?"

The bus came to a sudden stop. The old engine spit and hissed, and finally went quiet.

"Last stop—Smokey Joe's Ranch!" Smokey Joe called out in his best tour guide tenor. Then he nodded toward Arvin who was still fast asleep. "Harry, you ought to wake up Marvin there."

"Hey Arvin." Harry shook his shoulder. "Get up."

"Huh?" Arvin yawned and sat up. "Did I miss anything?"

Chapter 4

Wanted Poster and Stolen Money

The next morning, Harry, Gillian and Arvin woke up to the delicious smell of flapjacks and bacon.

"Rise and shine!" Smokey Joe hollered from the kitchen. "Chow's on! Come and git it!"

The kitchen could feed an army of ranch hands, but the long wooden table was set for only four. A huge, empty stew pot hung in an open fireplace. Dusty fry pans, some with cobwebs, hung from the rafters. They hadn't been used in ages.

Harry and Gillian came into the kitchen, slid onto the benches, and pulled them up close to the table. A scrumptious country breakfast sizzled on the plates in front of them.

"Morning Smokey Joe." Harry picked up a fork and speared a plump sausage.

"Morning," Gillian echoed as she reached for the maple syrup.

Smokey Joe lifted first one dusty boot, then the other over the wooden bench and plopped down in his usual spot. "Morning everybody. How did you green-horns sleep last night in that old bunkhouse? I hope the coyotes didn't keep you awake."

"Oh, no," Gillian said. "I couldn't close my eyes because..."

"...of Arvin's snoring. Isn't that right, Gillian?" Harry gave her a look.

"Uh, yeah." She stuffed her mouth with another fork full of flapjacks.

The door behind them creaked. Then Arvin pushed through in a hurry, untangling his twisted suspenders on the way. "Did I miss anything?" He wasn't about to lose out again like he had last night.

Smokey Joe handed him a plate. "Better grab some grub while the gettin's good. You're the last one to the trough, Marvin."

"That's *Arvin*," he said, as he started to pile on the pancakes. Then he turned to Harry. "Hey, how come you didn't wake me up on the bus last night when the ghost appeared? Tell me what happened."

"You had to be there Arvin," Harry said.

"But I *was* there."

"You were asleep!" Gillian said as she grabbed a piece of bacon just as Arvin reached for it.

Arvin gave her a dirty look. Then he saw the WANTED POSTERS on the counter. "Hey, is this the poster with the ghost on it?" He picked up the poster that had been on the front seat of the bus.

"Yup," Harry nodded.

Arvin read, "'Wanted: Dead Man Jack. Notorious train robber, bank robber and stage coach robber. Reward for bringing him in dead or alive.' Hey! We could still collect the reward. It says dead or alive."

Gillian groaned. "You can't collect a reward on a ghost."

"That reward's been paid out long ago," Smokey Joe said. "But you still might be able to rustle up a saddlebag full of money."

"Money?" Arvin's eyes lit up. "How?"

"We'll be taking the same authentic trail that outlaws used to escape from the sheriff and the posse," Smokey Joe explained. "Sometimes they hid their stolen money along the trail with the idea of coming back to get it later."

"And they didn't always make it back?" Gillian asked.

"Exactly," said Smokey Joe. "They say there's still a fortune out on the trail, just waiting to be found."

"Really..." The wheels in Arvin's head began to turn, but Gillian was the speed bump.

"Arvin, don't get any stupid ideas."

"How do you know it's stupid?"

"Arvin..."

"Wow!" Harry exclaimed. "This is going to be cool. How many cattle drives have you been on Smokey Joe?"

"Oh, I must have ridden this trail over a hundred times. Same time, every year. But this is the first time I ever brought greenhorns along," Smokey Joe chuckled.

Arvin scowled. He didn't like being called a greenhorn, even though he was one.

"Where's the end of the trail?" Gillian asked.

Smokey Joe unfolded a map and pointed to a spot. "See this on the map? It's the train station where we load the cattle. As a matter of fact, this is the same train station where a particular bounty hunter loaded up Dead Man Jack to turn him into the sheriff. That was a long time ago."

"Really?" Harry took a closer look.

Arvin glanced at the map and then sat back. "I knew that."

"You did not," Gillian snapped.

Smokey Joe continued. "The bounty hunter was none other than Silver Dollar Dan."

"Silver Dollar Dan." Harry was impressed. "Cool."

"Take a look at the trail on the map. We're driving these ill-tempered, longhorn cattle through wild and desolate country. It's dangerous business."

"Dangerous? Like how?" asked Arvin.

Smokey Joe let out a low whistle. "There's coyotes and rattle snakes. There's the blistering sun, blinding dust storms, and wild rivers to cross. Then sometimes, just sometimes, there's a double-crossing, thieving cowboy riding right along beside you. And you don't know it until it's too late."

They are interrupted by the clanking of pots and pans. Smokey Joe nodded toward the noise, "Our cook's loading up the wagon. You all met him on the bus, didn't you?"

The cook ambled toward them with his spurs jingling. He grumbled and snarled, "No good, no count, side winding pots and pans..."

Harry's eyes grew wide. "It's the Cowboy with the Silver Tooth!"

Chapter 5
Cattle Drive

Harry, Gillian and Arvin each saddled up one of the trail horses, with help from Smokey Joe. Gillian was the first to finish. She put one foot into her stirrup and tried to heave her other leg over the saddle. It took a few tries to make it on board, but finally she did. It wasn't easy for Arvin either. But lucky for him, Gillian was looking the other way. While the horses were used to cattle drives, the kids were not.

The cows mooed and moaned, bumping into each other and kicking up clouds of dust.

"Alright, then. Is everybody saddled up?" Smokey Joe asked. "Marvin, are you sure you can handle Bullet? He's a spry pony. If he gets spooked, he could run off with you."

Arvin sat up a little straighter in his saddle, "I've

ridden a lot of wild horses, I'm experienced. And that's Arvin, with an A."

"A for airhead," Gillian said with a smirk.

"Gillian, you don't have a clue." Arvin nudged his horse, and it easily followed Smokey Joe out onto the trail. Arvin turned and smiled smugly at Gillian.

But his smile faded when he saw that Gillian and Harry's horses did the exact same thing, as if by habit.

After a long, dusty day in the saddle, the group stopped and set up camp. Eerie, dark storm clouds covered the sky, with only a sliver of moon drifting in and out of the shadows. The horses were nervous.

It didn't take long to build a fire, lay out the bedrolls and pitch a tent. After they fed the horses, the group gathered around the crackling campfire to eat their supper. Coyotes howled in the distance.

As they wolfed down their sausage and beans, everyone talked about the day on the trail. That is, everyone except the Cowboy with the Silver Tooth. He ate in silence. When he was finished, he left without a word and started loading supplies into the tent.

Smokey Joe picked up his guitar and sang:

I hid my silver on this lonesome trail.
Three paces past the moon and a rusty nail.
But I got hung up with a noose.
I tried, but I couldn't get loose.

30

I never made it back.
Now they call me Dead Man Jack.

Dead Man Jack, never look back.
Dead Man Jack, never look back.

Smokey Joe put his guitar down, looked around, and sniffed the air. "Time for more firewood." He got up, brushed the dust off his pants, and headed into the darkness.

Arvin was restless. As soon as Smokey Joe was out of sight, he made a beeline toward the horses.

Gillian grabbed his sleeve. "Where are you going?"

"I'm going out to look around." He shook his sleeve until she let go.

"Arvin, you're not going to find any stolen money out there."

"You think you can read my mind?"

"What mind?"

"Gillian, if you ever got a clue, I'd be amazed."

There was a low rumbling of thunder in the distance. Arvin mounted Bullet on the first try, and disappeared into the dark night.

Chapter 6

Silver Dollar Dan and the Phantom

Smokey Joe threw two dry logs on the campfire. The hungry flames started to gnaw away at them, sending curly black smoke into the sky.

Smokey Joe studied the horizon. "Looks like there's a storm rolling in. I'll have to check on the horses in a bit. Horses don't like storms," he paused and took a deep breath, "except for the Phantom Horse."

"What's the Phantom Horse?" Gillian's eyes were wide.

Smokey Joe sat down, leaned his back against a big rock, and winced. After a day in the saddle, his creaky old spine needed some padding. He reached for a canvas bag and tucked it behind him for a pillow. Satisfied, he began his story. "When a bolt of lightning flickers through the sky, you can sometimes see her on that high bluff over there." He pointed in the distance. "The Phantom belonged to Silver Dollar Dan."

"The bounty hunter?" Harry asked.

"That's right," Smokey Joe nodded. "The Phantom was so black that she blended in with the night. So you never knew Silver Dollar Dan was on your trail...until it was too late."

"How did he capture the robbers?" Gillian asked.

Smokey Joe shook his head, "Oh, he was cunning. He waited until it was a cloudy night, without a star in the sky, like tonight. Then, Silver Dollar Dan crept into the robber's camp. He'd stand there in the pitch black night, and..."

Gillian leaned forward, "...and what?"

"Breathe," said Smokey Joe as he exhaled.

"Just breathe?" asked Harry.

"That's right," Smokey Joe replied, "You could smell his hot, cigar-smoking breath right over your head. His breath would rise like steam in the cold night air. But you still couldn't see him."

"What happened next?" asked Harry.

"Next, you would hear the coins. Silver Dollar Dan tossed coins in the palm of his hand because he liked the sound they made. Then he took one coin and scraped it across the side of the robber's saddlebags. That's usually where the stolen money was hidden. 'Silver finds silver,' he always said."

"Ooooh!" Gillian exclaimed. "Silver finds silver. That's creepy."

Smokey Joe continued. "At first, you would think it was only a tumbleweed brushing up against your saddlebag. Then the hair on the back of your neck would stand on end. Out of the pitch darkness you'd hear..."

"What?" Gillian asked.

"The Phantom. The Phantom would rear up on her hind legs, beating the air with her hooves."

"And the robber took off running?" Harry asked.

Smokey Joe nodded. "Yeah, but he didn't get far. Silver Dollar Dan would throw a lasso into the air, circling it around and around in the black sky. Then, like a giant invisible hand, the rope yanked the robber out of the darkness. With each tug of the rope, Silver Dollar Dan could hear the sound of his reward—silver dollars—jingling in the air."

"Wow..." Harry whistled. "Did Silver Dollar Dan get every man he went after?"

"Every man...except, except one." Smokey Joe coughed.

"Are you alright, Smokey Joe?" Gillian poured water from the canteen into a tin cup and passed it to him.

He sipped the water, a little dazed. "Yeah...yeah, I'm alright. Where's that Cowboy?"

A horse stomped and whinnied by the cook's wagon. Harry turned and pointed. "He's over there."

"He's getting on his horse...." Gillian said.

"He's outta here." Harry watched him ride toward the high bluffs. "I wonder where he's going?"

Smokey Joe stood up and gazed at the horizon. "I know where he's going."

"Arvin's out there too, riding Bullet," Gillian added.

"Ooooh, doggie," Smokey Joe said nervously. "He shouldn't be riding that skittish pony when there's a storm coming."

"That's Arvin for you." Gillian said. "He gets it in his head that he's going to find stolen money and he can't let go."

"He was chompin' at the bit," Smokey Joe said. "That's just the way you get when you're prospecting for silver coins."

Harry tried to coax Smokey Joe back to his campfire story. "Come on, Smokey Joe. Finish telling us about Silver Dollar Dan. Please?"

Smokey Joe was still watching the dark horizon. "This isn't a good night for anyone to be out on the bluffs. This night of all nights."

"What do you mean *this night*?" Gillian asked.

The wind whistled through the rocky canyons. A lone coyote howled.

Gillian and Harry moved closer to the campfire as a cold, clammy breeze swirled around them. The flames flickered and danced high in the air, casting eerie shadows on Smokey Joe's face. He looked very creepy.

Smokey Joe finished his water, put down his tin cup, and took a deep breath. Then he continued. "Silver Dollar Dan tracked Dead Man Jack for three long years. Every time Dan got close enough to feel the reward in his itchy palms, Jack outsmarted him.

"Then, 125 years ago tonight, Silver Dollar Dan spun a lasso around Jack. And since Dan figured the reward wouldn't be near enough to pay for all his years of tracking, he took the stolen money in Jack's saddlebags."

"Silver Dollar Dan stole the money that Dead Man Jack stole?" Harry was amazed.

"He sure did. Dan buried those silver dollars somewhere on this trail. Then he loaded Dead Man Jack into the train car to take him to the sheriff. But something happened in that train car...." Smokey Joe stopped abruptly.

A burst of thunder unleashed a storm cloud. "Ahh-hh!" Harry and Gillian were pelted with rain. They ran to the tent, but by the time they reached it, they were already soaked.

A thunderbolt ripped through the sky and the kids felt it rumble through the ground under their feet. It spooked the cattle and horses.

The frantic whinny of one horse rose up above all the others. It came from a bluff way off in the distance. It took a moment for Harry's eyes to focus through the dark, rainy night. Then he saw it. It was black, and it was moving. "Look up on that rock! It's a black horse beating its hooves in the air!"

A streak of lightening flickered across the sky and surrounded the horse.

Gillian cried out, "It's...it's the Phantom!"

Chapter 7

What's Outside the Tent?

The storm finally died down. Harry and Gillian huddled around a gas lantern in the supply tent. They were the only ones left in camp. The cows moaned around them and coyotes howled in the distance.

Gillian hugged her knees and stared wide-eyed at the lantern. "I'm scared, Harry. That Phantom Horse is a ghost. We saw it because something happened over a hundred years ago tonight, and we don't know what it is!"

A vulture screeched and Harry shuddered. "This whole thing is giving me the creeps."

"Smokey Joe's been out there looking for Arvin for a long time," she said as she bit her thumbnail. "They should have been back by now."

"Maybe Smokey Joe's not looking for Arvin," Harry said.

"What do you mean?" Gillian asked.

"Maybe he's looking for buried money too."

"Harry..."

"Remember, he said he's ridden this trail over a hundred times, the same time every year."

Gillian stopped and thought a moment. Then she said what they were both thinking. "Smokey Joe's not a ghost, is he?"

Harry shook his head. "I don't know. I don't think so. But he sure knows a lot of creepy stuff."

"What about the Cowboy with the Silver Tooth?" Gillian asked.

"He's no cook, that's for sure."

"Then what is he?"

Suddenly, they heard the sound of something scraping on canvas. Gillian jerked her head around. "What's that?"

Harry listened. "Something's scraping on our tent. It's pitch black out there. I can't see a thing."

"It sounds like a coin," Gillian whispered. "Silver finds silver..."

Harry turned quickly toward Gillian. "Put out the lantern."

"Why?"

Harry grabbed the lantern and blew out the flame. "He can see us through the tent."

"Who can see us?" A soft wind blew up around them. Gillian moved toward the center of the tent. "Is that... breathing?

"No, it's the wind," Harry assured her.

The gust of wind circled the tent. When it swirled around a second time, it turned into loud, eerie breathing that filled the night air. Gillian shrieked, "It's breathing!!!"

Harry opened the tent flap and pulled Gillian out. They ran screaming into the dark night. "Aaahh!!"

Their footsteps pounded against the wet ground. They ran way past the point of exhaustion, too scared to slow down. But finally, gulping and gasping for air, Harry and Gillian stumbled to a stop.

"It's so dark. I can't see where we're going. Gillian, are you there?" Harry asked breathlessly.

"Yeah, I'm right behind you. Harry, listen. It sounds like vultures!"

Harry panted. "Vultures! That means...oh, no!"

The birds screeched and flapped their wings as they swooped toward the ground looking for prey.

Thunder rumbled, and lightning flickered through the sky, showing a steep, rocky drop in front of them.

"Look out!" Gillian cried. "It's a cliff!"

Harry looked around, fearing the worst. Then he hollered, "Arvin! Smokey Joe! Anybody! Can you hear me?" His voice echoed in the canyon below, then faded into silence.

Out of the dark night, they heard rattling. "Listen," Gillian whispered. "Don't move, Harry. It's a rattle snake."

"No, it's not a rattler," Harry said. "It's coins. Someone's tossing coins. And it's getting closer."

"And closer," Gillian said softly.

Chapter 8
Double Cross

The sound of coins jingling in the air suddenly stopped. Gillian and Harry looked toward the hazy bluff, expecting to see something—but nothing was there.

Then, out of the darkness, they heard singing.

I hid my silver on this lonesome trail.
Three paces past the moon and a rusty nail.
But I got hung up with a noose.
I tried, but I couldn't get loose.
I never made it back.
Now they call me Dead Man Jack.

Dead Man Jack, never look back.
Dead Man Jack, never look back.

At the end of the song, they heard the old Prospector's eerie laugh. It was the same Prospector whose face had been floating in the bus's windshield.

Then they heard, but couldn't see, the Cowboy with the Silver Tooth. He growled and snarled at the Prospector, just like he did in the bus. "Where did you hide my money? You no good, double-crossing, smelly old piece of vulture bait!"

The Prospector laughed again. "Who double-crossed who?"

"You stole my money from my saddlebag, you thieving old bounty hunter," the Cowboy bellowed.

"It wasn't your money, you smelly old bandit! The bounty on you wasn't near enough. I *earned* that money." The Prospector was riled up now.

Just then, the Prospector and Cowboy appeared on the bluff. They were faint at first, then became just as clear and plain as they were on the bus.

Harry finally understood. "The Prospector is the bounty hunter, Silver Dollar Dan!"

Gillian nodded. "And the Cowboy is Dead Man Jack!"

"Shhhh. Listen," Harry whispered.

"I've told you every year for 125 years, never steal from a thief!" Dead Man Jack hollered.

"I've told you every year for 125 years, never double-cross a bounty hunter!" Silver Dollar Dan shouted back.

Dead Man Jack laughed, "Oh, but I got you good! When you fell asleep in the train car, taking me in to the sheriff..."

Silver Dollar Dan interrupted, "I don't need to hear your gloat."

"I took my WANTED POSTER and shaded my silver hair to make it look black like yours..." continued Dead Man Jack.

"You never tire of your own yappin' do you?" Silver Dollar Dan pointed a grubby finger at the thief.

"Then I shaded in my silver hat to make it black like yours," Dead Man Jack continued.

"You ain't gonna get my goat," Silver Dollar Dan snapped. He was tired of hearing the story of how his last bounty hunting job ended.

"It was a fine piece of work. You should have been there," teased Dead Man Jack.

"I was there!" protested Silver Dollar Dan.

"You were asleep!" Dead Man Jack grinned with delight as he remembered his cleverness. "Then I reached down and plucked one of the silver spokes off my spurs and used it for my missing tooth. So you were the only toothless one in the train car! You looked just like my WANTED POSTER!"

"When the doors of the train swung open," said Silver Dollar Dan, "you held up that poster and pointed at me. I didn't even get a chance to wipe the sleep out of my eyes before the sheriff threw a noose 'round my neck and strung me up."

"Yeah," said Dead Man Jack, satisfied. "The sheriff strung up the bounty hunter and let the thief go free!"

"Oh, but I had the last laugh, didn't I?" Silver Dollar Dan sneered at him.

"You went prospecting in my saddlebags! Then hid my money so I can't find it! For 125 years I've been traipsing this trail looking for my money." Dead Man Jack snarled at the bounty hunter.

"If you ever got the clue, I'd be amazed."

"But you didn't utter a clue," said Dead Man Jack. "You wasted your last snake's breath singing some lame brain song."

"Harry, that's it!" Gillian cried out. "The clue to finding the buried money is in the song!"

"I don't remember the words," Harry said.

"I do." Gillian recited, "I hid my silver on this lonesome trail. Three paces past the moon and a rusty nail."

Harry was puzzled. "What does that mean?"

"Look!" Gillian pointed. "The moon is coming out from behind the storm clouds. It's shining a beam of light—where is it hitting?"

"That tree." Harry followed the beam of light with his finger. "It's awfully close to the cliff..."

"Look!" Gillian exclaimed. "Somebody pounded a nail in this old tree!"

"And the shadow from the nail is almost like a finger pointing to..." Harry was interrupted by the sudden appearance of the Phantom Horse. She stomped and whinnied, and pounded her hooves at the dirt.

"The Phantom is on the bluff!" Gillian hollered.

The very spot!" Harry cried. "The Phantom is pounding the dirt and uncovering..."

Silver Dollar Dan chided Dead Man Jack. "You are the stupid one, aren't you?"

"Why you four flushing, side winding..." Dead Man Jack muttered.

"You egg sucker..." Silver Dollar Dan gave it right back to him.

"I don't know why I put up with you all these years, you old vulture bait," said Dead Man Jack. "I'm going to get my money if it's the last thing I do!"

"Stay away from those silver coins, you double-crossing outlaw!" hollered Silver Dollar Dan.

Dead Man Jack jumped in front of the pile of dirt. "They're *my* silver coins!"

"They're *my* silver coins!" cried the bounty hunter.

Suddenly, they were interrupted by the sound of pounding hooves. A horse was speeding right toward them!

Chapter 9

Found and Lost

"Whoa Bullet! Slow down Bullet! Help! Help! Runaway horse!! Somebody do something!!" The dust billowed around the galloping horse, hiding the rider. But the voice was unmistakable.

"It's Arvin!" Gillian cried out. "Pull on the reins!"

"Arvin, try to jump off!" Harry hollered, hoping Arvin could hear him above the deafening sound of the pounding hooves.

"Get out of the way everybody! I can't stop!"

"Arvin jump! Hurry! You're headed toward the cliff!! Get off, Arvin! Now!" Harry ran after him as fast as he could. But he couldn't outrun a spooked horse.

"Aaahh!!!" Arvin hung on for dear life as he sped

toward the hundred-foot drop into the cavern.

"Hold on there, Marvin! I've got you!" Smokey Joe shouted. He galloped behind Arvin, spinning his lasso in the air. Just before Arvin reached the edge of the cliff near the Phantom Horse, the lasso dropped around Bullet and Arvin. Bullet slid to a stop, pushing the silver coins over the side of the cliff into the cavern below.

"Oh no!" Gillian said softly.

Harry looked down into the cavern. "All that money!"

Dead Man Jack appeared again. "My money! It's at the bottom of the canyon!"

Silver Dollar Dan stood next to him chuckling. "After all these years, who would've thought…"

"Dadburn it! It was jest finding its way back into my saddlebags."

Silver Dollar Dan shook his head, almost calmly. "It's a lowdown lizard's luck."

"My silver dollars are gone for good." Dead Man Jack gave the canyon one last look.

Silver Dollar Dan looked sideways at Jack. "Now you don't have to look for 'em no more."

Dead Man Jack stepped back and narrowed his eyes at Silver Dollar Dan. "So you think we're squared up now?"

"I didn't say we were squared up."

"You're spoutin' off like we're squared up."

Just then, the whistling wind swirled around them.

Silver Dollar Dan looked into the distance, his eyes were softer, more mellow. "Hey, that wind's blowin' in a different direction."

"You're right. It surely is," Dead Man Jack said quietly. "I think it's time to move camp, Dan. What d'ya say?"

"Yup. Looks like we're at the end of this trail, Jack. Phantom? Are you comin'?"

The Phantom whinnied in response.

Chapter 10

End of the Trail

"Arvin, let me give you a hand." Harry reached up to Arvin, who was still holding tight to Bullet's saddle horn.

"Arvin, are you okay?" Gillian asked.

Arvin got off the horse, a little shaken. "Uh, yeah. Ah, sure." Then he turned to Gillian with a smile, "You actually figured out that clue, I'm amazed. I'm glad I didn't miss it."

"Thanks. And you weren't that bad riding Bullet. I thought you'd be worse," she said, returning the compliment.

"Thanks." Arvin brushed off his dusty pants. He felt pretty proud of himself.

Smokey Joe clapped his hands together. "Well, is everybody ready to head back to camp?"

The kids nodded and started walking toward the

smoldering campfire in the distance. Harry looked back at the horizon and the cliff. "That was a...a..."

"A little delay," Smokey Joe interrupted. "We'll be back on the trail first thing in the morning. It's the same, authentic trail used by outlaws, desperadoes and cattle rustlers over 100 years ago. Yup, we'll start driving these ill-tempered, longhorn cattle through wild and desolate country. There's coyotes and rattle snakes. There's the blistering sun, blinding dust storms, and wild rivers to cross. Then sometimes, just sometimes, there's a double-crossing, thieving cowboy riding right along beside you. And you don't know it until it's too late."

In the distance, they hear the voices of Dead Man Jack and Silver Dollar Dan singing together:

> I hid my silver on this lonesome trail.
> Three paces past the moon and a rusty nail.
>
> But I got hung up with a noose.
> I tried, but I couldn't get loose.
> I never made it back.
> Now they call me Dead Man Jack.
>
> Dead Man Jack, never look back.
> Dead Man Jack, never look back.

THE END

It's time to create
your own
Movie for the Ear.

(Squeaky door sound here.)

Come on in.

(Foot tapping here.)

Holly is waiting for you.

Create Your Own
Movie for the Ear®

Hello, I'm Holly!

I've spent a little time in Hollywood, so I know talent when I see it. That's why I know you will be terrific as one of the stars in your own Movie for the Ear!

A Movie for the Ear is all about SOUND. You act out your part with your VOICE. You read the lines the way your character would say them. Have fun creating SOUND EFFECTS. You can even add MUSIC!

Here's how to get started:

1. Cast the Roles
Haunted Cattle Drive is full of juicy parts you can really sink your teeth into.

You can read the entire script aloud, or you can divide the roles with one other person. I do that all the time when I'm rehearsing for a part.

For a full Movies for the Ear production, cast your classmates, friends, or family in the roles. Remember, actors can play more than one part. They just have to use a different voice for each character. You'll get the hang of it.

2. Rehearse
Your director will organize and oversee your rehearsals. Make sure everyone is comfortable with their lines before adding sound effects or music.

3. Sound Effects (SFX)
Go through the script and note the items labeled "SFX." That stands for sound effects. Mark a few that you would like to try. Then have fun finding creative ways to make the sounds.

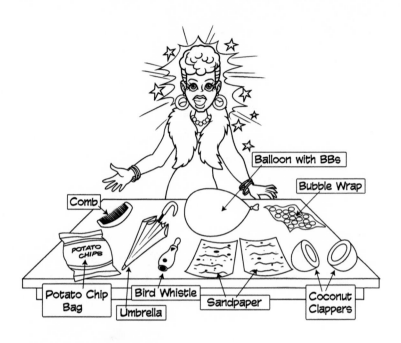

Here are some examples:

Balloon with BBs inside . . . . Thunder
Coconut halves . . . . Horse trotting
Sandpaper . . . . Train engine
Cellophane Potato Chip Bag . . . . . . Fire crackling
Run thumb across comb teeth . . . . Crickets
Snap bubble wrap . . . . Wood snapping in fire
Umbrella . . . . Flapping wings
Bird whistle . . . . Bird caws

Choose one or two people to be your sound effects
artists.

4. Music
Find a short piece of music to play at the beginning of your production.

Find an instrumental piece to play at the end while your narrator reads your "credit roll." That means your narrator will announce the names of the actors and the parts they played. Also include the names of your director, sound effects artists, music director, and anyone else who worked on your production.

If you would like, you can include other short pieces of music throughout your Movie for the Ear.

5. Make a Poster
Download the poster template from the website, www.creepersmysteries.com. Customize it for your own production, and use it to invite your audience.

Now, go have a blast! I'll be listening...

—Holly

CREEPERS® Mysteries

Haunted Cattle Drive
Movie for the Ear Script

By Connie Kingrey Anderson

Movies for the Ear®

CREEPERS® Mysteries
Haunted Cattle Drive

Cast & Crew

Production Company _____

Director _____

Ebeneezer Stump/Narrator _____

Harry _____

Gillian _____

Arvin _____

Cowboy with the Silver Tooth _____

Toothless Old Prospector _____

Silver Dollar Dan, the Bounty Hunter _____

Dead Man Jack, the Thief _____

Sound Effects Artist #1 _____

Sound Effects Artist #2 _____

Music Director _____

CREEPERS Mysteries
Haunted Cattle Drive
Movie for the Ear Script

MUSIC: CREEPERS THEME SONG

SFX: FOOTSTEPS, KEYS JINGLING, LOCK TURNING. Old Wooden DOOR CREAKING OPEN.

EBENEEZER: Hello, come in. I'm Ebeneezer Stump. And you are? Oh, I see. Hmmm... You are here for a Creepers Mystery...

SFX: COYOTE HOWLS ECHO through the canyon. OWLS HOOT

EBENEEZER: Have you ever gathered around a cowboy's campfire on a pitch black night? And felt like someone was standing beside you in the dark? Have you ever heard scratching on the side of your tent, and hoped it was only a tumbleweed? (laughter) Get ready for this episode of *Creepers Mysteries*. Here it comes... Haunted Cattle Drive!

ACT I, SCENE 1

SFX: ENGINE TURNS OVER. A SQUEAKY BUS RATTLES over a dirt road.

SMOKEY JOE: Howdy everybody, I'm Smokey Joe. Just sit back and enjoy the bus ride out to my ranch. Feast your eyes on cowpoke country. Now, what did you say your names were?

HARRY: I'm Harry, and this is my sister Gillian.

GILLIAN: Hi.

SMOKEY JOE: I like to check out everybody I haul out to Smokey Joe's Ranch, just to see if they match any pictures on the WANTED POSTERS. Don't want you sliding up to a can of beans at my table, only to find out you're a couple of low down, no good varmints.

HARRY: Our mom's travel agency is going to start booking vacations on your ranch, so we're trying it out for her.

ARVIN: Hey...

HARRY: Oh, and this is Arvin.

ARVIN: I can introduce myself. (to Smokey Joe) I'm Arvin.

SMOKEY JOE: I thought only two city slickers were coming out here to get prickly burrs in their britches, Marvin.

ARVIN: That's Arvin. And yeah, *they're* the two city slickers. *I'm* an experienced horseman.

GILLIAN: Arvin thinks he's an expert, but he's only the extra ticket. Buy two, get one free.

ARVIN: Gillian, your mom *begged* me to come along because you don't have a clue.

GILLIAN: (ignoring him) We still have to pay tax and destination charges. But otherwise, Arvin's free.

ACT I, SCENE 2

GILLIAN: Hey, Harry! (trying to get his attention) Hellooooo. What are you doing?

HARRY: Shhhh. Look.

GILLIAN: At what?

HARRY: There's a cowboy in the back of the bus, and there's something really weird about him.

GILLIAN: What cowboy?

HARRY: In the last seat. He's got a silver hat, silver hair and silver tooth.

GILLIAN: There's nobody back there, Harry. Turn around.

HARRY: Hey! He's gone!

GILLIAN: There's no place to go on a moving bus.

HARRY: (spooked) But, he was there. How could he have disappeared into thin air?

ARVIN: (know-it-all) Thin air is common in high altitudes, Harry. There's less air getting to your brain.

GILLIAN: You should know airhead.

ACT I, SCENE 3

SFX: SQUEAKY BUS RATTLES, WIND WHISTLES, COYOTE HOWLS

EBENEEZER: It's a long, lonely road out to Smokey Joe's Ranch. The wind whistles through the bluffs, and tumbleweeds skitter across the deserted road. The day drifts into a cold, pitch black night. The bus headlights snake their way through the darkness.

SFX: COINS CLINK against each other. The CLINKING starts in the distance, then gets closer and closer.

GILLIAN: (whispering) Harry, what's that?

HARRY: Is it Arvin?

GILLIAN: No, he's asleep.

HARRY: It sounds like someone tossing coins.

GILLIAN: But where's it coming from?

HARRY: I don't know.

GILLIAN: It's getting closer.

HARRY: It's so dark I can't see a thing.

GILLIAN: We're the only ones on the bus.

HARRY: Except for that cowboy.

GILLIAN: There's no cowboy, Harry!

HARRY: Maybe it's Smokey Joe...

GILLIAN: No, he's driving the bus.

HARRY: Yeah, and the sound's getting closer...

GILLIAN: ...and closer. This is really creepy, Harry. I'm scared...

SFX: COIN TOSSING increases in speed and volume.

SMOKEY JOE: (hollering) AAAHH! Get outta the way!

SFX: BUS BRAKES SCREECH. BUS CLUNKS to a stop.

EBENEEZER: Smokey Joe loses control of the bus. It skids, and then lands in a ditch.

GILLIAN: Aaahh! There's a face in the windshield!

HARRY: Man alive!

GILLIAN: (frightened) No, he's not. Look!

HARRY: It's just a face—and it's floating!

PROSPECTOR: (laughs) Dead Man Jack, never look back. Dead Man Jack, never look back. (laughs)

EBENEEZER: It's a Prospector from the old Gold Rush days. He has black hair, a black hat and a big toothless grin.

Suddenly, the Cowboy with the Silver Tooth appears. He slowly slithers up from behind the last seat in the bus. He pushes up the brim of his silver hat and squints his eyes at the Prospector.

EBENEEZER: The Cowboy slowly walks down the aisle of the bus, his spurs jingling with every step. He plants his boots squarely in front of the windshield.

SFX: Slow, heavy BOOT FOOTSTEPS with SPURS JINGLING.

COWBOY: Why you no count, good for nothin' silver mining thief...I'll teach you to go prospecting in my saddlebags!

PROSPECTOR: (laughter) You think you can take me, you double-crossing snake? Eyeball to eyeball?

COWBOY: Eyeball to eyeball. (growls) I'll stare you down if it's the last thing I do.

SFX: STARING SOUND EFFECT

PROSPECTOR: (laughter) You forget, I've got the beadiest eyes in the West.

SFX: COUNTER STARE

EBENEEZER: The Prospector glares back at the Cowboy with eyes so hot they almost sizzle. The Cowboy becomes weak and drenched in sweat.

COWBOY: (snarling, gasping for air) I'll get you, you stinkin' Prospector, you low down lizard...

EBENEEZER: The Cowboy struggles to pull a small box of matches from his pocket. He strikes one match and holds it in front of his shiny silver tooth.

SFX: MATCH STRIKING, then RICOCHET SOUNDS.

EBENEEZER: The light ricochets off the silver tooth and shoots toward the windshield. The beam *blasts* away at the Prospector's floating face.

SFX: BLAST!

PROSPECTOR: Aaahh!!

EBENEEZER: When the Cowboy blows out the match...

SFX: DISAPPEARING STING

EBENEEZER: ...the Prospector is gone.

HARRY: Did you see that?

GILLIAN: (scared) What was it?

HARRY: (scared) I think it was a...a...

SFX: BUS ENGINE TURNS OVER

SMOKEY JOE: ...A slight delay. Just a slight delay. Are you kids alright? I had a sudden turn there. But we'll be on our way again in no time.

HARRY: Smokey Joe, who was that in the window?

SMOKEY JOE: *Who?* You mean *what.* A big old tumbleweed was what it was, Harry. Rolled smack across the windshield.

HARRY: No, it was a toothless old Prospector. He had black hair and a black hat.

GILLIAN: And his face was floating!

SMOKEY JOE: Now, you kids are lettin' your imaginations run away with you like a couple of broncos that ain't been broke yet.

HARRY: He said "Dead Man Jack, never look back."

SMOKEY JOE: Dead Man Jack? Oh, you must have been dreaming about those WANTED POSTERS over there on the front seat. There it is, right on the top.

SFX: PAPER RUSTLING

HARRY: Hey, Gillian, look at this poster. (reading) Wanted: Dead Man Jack. Notorious train robber, bank robber and stage coach robber. Bounty Hunters Welcome.

GILLIAN: That's the guy alright.

SMOKEY JOE: You kids forget that the poster is over 100 years old.

HARRY: So the guy we saw is....

SMOKEY JOE: Dead. Dead as a doornail.

GILLIAN: So that floating face was...a ghost?

SFX: BUS comes to a stop. ENGINE is switched off.

SMOKEY JOE: Last stop—Smokey Joe's Ranch. Harry, you ought to wake up Marvin there.

HARRY: Hey, Arvin.

ARVIN: (yawning) Did I miss anything?

ACT II, SCENE 1

SFX: ROOSTER CROWS. BACON SIZZLES.

EBENEEZER: The next morning, Harry, Gillian and Arvin wake up to the delicious smell of flapjacks and bacon.

SMOKEY JOE: (shouting) Rise and shine! Chow's on! Come and get it!

SFX: DOOR OPENING

HARRY: Morning, Smokey Joe.

GILLIAN: Morning.

SMOKEY JOE: Morning everybody. How did you greenhorns sleep last night in that old bunkhouse? I hope the coyotes didn't keep you awake.

GILLIAN: Oh, no. I couldn't close my eyes because...

HARRY: ...of Arvin's snoring. Isn't that right, Gillian?

GILLIAN: Uh, yeah.

SFX: DOOR OPENS

ARVIN: Did I miss anything?

SMOKEY JOE: Better grab some grub while the gettin's good. You're the last one to the trough, Marvin.

ARVIN: That's *Arvin*. (shift) Hey, Harry, how come you didn't wake me up on the bus last night when the ghost appeared? Tell me what happened.

HARRY: You had to be there Arvin.

ARVIN: But I *was* there.

GILLIAN: You were asleep!

SFX: CRINKLING PAPER

ARVIN: Hey, is this the poster with the ghost on it?

HARRY: Yup.

ARVIN: (reading) "Wanted: Dead Man Jack. Notorious train robber, bank robber and stage coach robber. Reward for bringing him in Dead or Alive." Hey! We could still collect the reward. It says dead or alive.

GILLIAN: You can't collect a reward on a ghost.

SMOKEY JOE: That reward's been paid out long ago. But you still might be able to rustle up a saddlebag full of money.

ARVIN: Money? How?

SMOKEY JOE: We'll be taking the same authentic trail that outlaws used to escape from the sheriff and the posse. Sometimes they hid their stolen money along the trail with the idea of coming back to get it later.

GILLIAN: And they didn't always make it back?

SMOKEY JOE: Exactly. They say there's still a fortune out on the trail, just waiting to be found.

ARVIN: Really...

GILLIAN: Arvin, don't get any stupid ideas.

ARVIN: How do you know it's stupid?

GILLIAN: Arvin...

HARRY: Wow! This is going to be cool. How many cattle drives have you been on Smokey Joe?

SMOKEY JOE: Oh, I must have ridden this trail over a 100 times. Same time every year. But this is the first time I ever brought greenhorns along.

GILLIAN: Where's the end of the trail?

SFX: MAP UNFOLDING

SMOKEY JOE: See this on the map? That's the train station where we load the cattle. As a matter of fact, this is the same train station where a particular bounty hunter loaded up Dead Man Jack to turn him into the sheriff.

HARRY: Really?

ARVIN: I knew that.

GILLIAN: You did not.

SMOKEY JOE: The bounty hunter was none other than Silver Dollar Dan.

HARRY: Silver Dollar Dan. Cool.

SMOKEY JOE: Take a look at the trail on the map. We're driving these ill-tempered, longhorn cattle through wild and desolate country. It's dangerous business.

ARVIN: Dangerous? Like how?

SMOKEY JOE: There's coyotes and rattle snakes. There's the blistering sun, blinding dust storms, and wild rivers to cross. Then sometimes, just sometimes, there's a double-crossing, thieving cowboy riding right along beside you. And you don't know it until it's too late.

SFX: POTS and PANS CLANKING

SMOKEY JOE: Here comes our cook. You all met him on the bus, didn't you?

SFX: BOOTS WALKING with JINGLING SPURS

COWBOY: (grumbling, snarling) No good, no count, side-winding pots and pans...

HARRY: It's the Cowboy with the Silver Tooth!

ACT II, SCENE 2

SFX: HORSES WHINNY, COWS MOO

SMOKEY JOE: Alright, then. Everybody's saddled up?

KIDS: Yup. Yeah.

SMOKEY JOE: Marvin, are you sure you can handle Bullet? He's a spry pony. If he gets spooked, he could run off with you.

ARVIN: I've ridden a lot of wild horses, I'm experienced. And that's Arvin, with an A.

GILLIAN: A for airhead.

ARVIN: Gillian, you don't have a clue.

ACT II, SCENE 3

SFX: HORSES WHINNY, COWS MOO

EBENEEZER: After a long, dusty day in the saddle, the group stops and sets up camp. Eerie, dark storm clouds cover the sky, with only a sliver of moon drifting in and out of the shadows. The horses are nervous.

MUSIC: MOOD MUSIC

EBENEEZER: It didn't take long to build a fire, lay out the bedrolls and pitch a tent.

SFX: FIRE CRACKLES. COYOTES HOWL in the distance.

EBENEEZER: Everyone's gathered around the campfire, eating their sausage and beans. The Cowboy with the Silver Tooth finishes, then goes to load supplies into the tent. Smokey Joe picks up his guitar.

SMOKEY JOE: (singing)
    I hid my silver on this lonesome trail.
    Three paces past the moon and a rusty nail.
    But I got hung up with a noose.
    I tried, but I couldn't get loose.
    I never made it back.
    Now they call me Dead Man Jack.

Dead Man Jack, never look back.
Dead Man Jack, never look back.

ARVIN: Can I be excused? I'm going to go out and look around.

GILLIAN: Arvin, you're not going to find any stolen money out there.

ARVIN: You think you can read my mind?

GILLIAN: What mind?

ARVIN: Gillian, if you could ever get a clue, I'd be amazed.

SFX: FOOTSTEPS RUNNING AWAY.

ACT II, SCENE 4

SFX: LOW RUMBLING OF THUNDER

SMOKEY JOE: Looks like there's a storm rolling in. I'll have to check on the horses in a bit. Horses don't like storms. (Shift) Except for the Phantom Horse.

GILLIAN: What's the Phantom Horse?

SMOKEY JOE: When a bolt of lightning flickers through the sky, you can sometimes see her on that high bluff over there. The Phantom belonged to Silver Dollar Dan.

HARRY: The bounty hunter!

SMOKEY JOE: That's right. The Phantom was so black she blended in with the night. So you never knew Silver Dollar Dan was on your trail...until it was too late.

GILLIAN: How did he capture the robbers?

SMOKEY JOE: He was cunning. He waited until it was a cloudy night, without a star in the sky—like tonight. Then, Silver Dollar Dan crept into the robber's camp. He'd stand there in the pitch black night, and...

GILLIAN: And what?

SMOKEY JOE: (exhales) Breathe.

HARRY: Just breathe?

SMOKEY JOE: That's right. You could smell his hot, cigar-smoking breath right over your head. His breath would rise like steam in the cold night air. But you still couldn't see him.

HARRY: What happened next?

SMOKEY JOE: Next, you would hear the coins.

SFX: COINS CLINKING

SMOKEY JOE: Silver Dollar Dan tossed coins in the palm of his hand because he liked the sound they made. Then he took one coin and scraped it across the side of the robber's saddlebags. That's usually where the stolen money was hidden.

SFX: SCRAPING SOUND with EERIE MUSIC

SMOKEY JOE: "Silver finds silver," he always said.

GILLIAN & HARRY: OOOOOHH!

GILLIAN: Silver finds silver. That's creepy.

SMOKEY JOE: At first, you would think it was only a tumbleweed brushing up against your saddlebag. Then the hair on the back of your neck would stand on end. Out of the pitch darkness you heard...

GILLIAN: What?

SFX: HORSE HOOVES STOMPING slowly.

SMOKEY JOE: The Phantom...

SFX: THUNDER CRACKLES, HORSE WHINNIES & SNORTS

SMOKEY JOE: The Phantom would rear up on her hind legs, beating the air with her hooves.

SFX: FEET RUNNING

HARRY: And the robber took off running?

SFX: LASSO CIRCLING IN THE AIR

SMOKEY JOE: Yeah, but he didn't get far. Silver Dollar Dan would throw a lasso into the air, circling it around and around in the black sky. Then...like a giant invisible hand, the rope yanked the robber out of the darkness.

GILLIAN: (small scream) Ooooh!

SMOKEY JOE: With each tug of the rope, Silver Dollar Dan could hear the sound of his reward—silver dollars—jingling in the air.

SFX: JINGLING increases in volume, then abruptly stops.

HARRY: Wow... Did Silver Dollar Dan get every man he went after?

SMOKEY JOE: Every man...except, except one. (coughs)

GILLIAN: Are you alright, Smokey Joe?

SMOKEY JOE: (a little dazed) Yeah...yeah, I'm alright. Where's that Cowboy?

SFX: HORSE STOMPS and WHINNIES.

HARRY: He's over there, by the horses.

GILLIAN: He's getting on his horse....

SFX: GALLOPING

HARRY: He's outta here.

GILLIAN: I wonder where he's going?

EBENEEZER: Smokey Joe watches the Cowboy as he rides out toward the high bluffs.

SMOKEY JOE: I know where he's going.

GILLIAN: Arvin's out there too, riding Bullet.

SMOKEY JOE: Ooooh, doggie. He shouldn't be riding that skittish pony when there's a storm coming.

GILLIAN: That's Arvin for you. He gets it in his head that he's going to find stolen money and he can't let it go.

SMOKEY JOE: (pointedly) He was chompin' at the bit. And that's just the way you get when you're prospecting for silver coins.

HARRY: Come on, Smokey Joe. Finish telling us about Silver Dollar Dan. Please?

SMOKEY JOE: (hushed) This isn't a good night for anyone to be out on the bluffs. This night of all nights.

GILLIAN: What do you mean *this* night?

SFX: WHISTLING WIND

EBENEEZER: Gillian and Harry move closer to the campfire as a cold, clammy breeze swirls around them. The flames flicker and dance high in the air, casting eerie shadows on Smokey Joe's face. He looks very creepy.

SMOKEY JOE: Silver Dollar Dan tracked Dead Man Jack for three long years. Every time Dan got close enough to feel the reward in his itchy palms, Jack outsmarted him.

Then, 125 years ago tonight, Silver Dollar Dan spun a lasso around Jack. And since Dan figured the reward wouldn't be near enough to pay for all his years of tracking, he took the stolen money in Jack's saddlebags.

HARRY: Silver Dollar Dan stole the money that Dead Man Jack stole?

SMOKEY JOE: He sure did. Dan buried those silver dollars somewhere on this trail, then he loaded Dead Man Jack on the train car to take him in to the sheriff. But something happened in that train car....

SFX: THUNDER BOLT, PELTING RAIN

HARRY & GILLIAN: Aaahh!

SMOKEY JOE: Quick, run to the tent before you're soaked.

HARRY: Come on, Gillian run! Fast!

GILLIAN: I am! I am!

SFX: FRIGHTENED HORSES & COWS, RAIN, THUNDER CRACKLES, HORSE WHINNIES

HARRY: Look up on that rock! It's a black horse beating its hooves in the air!

GILLIAN: It's...It's the Phantom!

ACT III, SCENE 1

EBENEEZER: The storm finally dies down. Harry and Gillian huddle around a gas lantern in the supply tent. They're the only ones left in camp.

SFX: COYOTES HOWL, COWS MOAN

GILLIAN: I'm scared. That Phantom Horse is a ghost. We saw it because something happened over a 100 years ago tonight—and we don't know what it is!

SFX: VULTURE SCREECHES

HARRY: This is giving me the creeps.

GILLIAN: Smokey Joe's been out there looking for Arvin for a long time. They should have been back by now.

HARRY: Maybe Smokey Joe's not looking for Arvin.

GILLIAN: What do you mean?

HARRY: Maybe he's looking for buried money too.

GILLIAN: Harry...

HARRY: Remember, he said he's ridden this trail over 100 times, the same time every year.

GILLIAN: Smokey Joe's not a ghost. Is he?

HARRY: I don't think so. But he sure knows a lot of creepy stuff.

GILLIAN: What about the Cowboy with the Silver Tooth?

HARRY: He's no cook, that's for sure.

GILLIAN: Then what is he?

SFX: SCRAPING on canvas

GILLIAN: (gasp) What's that?

HARRY: Something's scraping on our tent. It's pitch black out there. I can't see a thing.

GILLIAN: It sounds like a coin.

HARRY: Silver finds silver... Gillian, put out the lantern.

GILLIAN: Why?

HARRY: He can see us through the tent.

GILLIAN: Who can see us?

SFX: SOFT WIND BLOWING

GILLIAN: Is that...breathing?

HARRY: No, it's the wind.

SFX: WIND BLOWING/BREATHING...

GILLIAN: No, it's breathing!

HARRY: Let's get out of here!

GILLIAN & HARRY: Aaahh!!!!

ACT III, SCENE 2

SFX: FOOTSTEPS RUNNING

HARRY: (panting) Gillian, are you there?

GILLIAN: (panting) Yeah, I'm right behind you.

HARRY: (panting) It's so dark. I can't see where we're going.

SFX: COYOTES HOWL, VULTURES SCREECH & WINGS FLAP

GILLIAN: (panting) Harry, it sounds like vultures!

HARRY: (panting) Vultures! That means...oh, no!

SFX: THUNDER, RUNNING stops

GILLIAN: Look out! It's a cliff!

HARRY: Arvin! Smokey Joe! Anybody! Can you hear me?

GILLIAN: Listen! Don't move, Harry. It's a rattle snake.

SFX: COINS BEING TOSSED

HARRY: No, it's not a rattle snake. It's coins.

GILLIAN: And it's getting closer.

HARRY: And closer.

ACT III, SCENE 3

PROSPECTOR: (singing)
    I hid my silver on this lonesome trail.
    Three paces past the moon and a rusty nail.
    But I got hung up with a noose.
    I tried, but I couldn't get loose.
    I never made it back.
    Now they call me Dead Man Jack.

    Dead Man Jack, never look back.
    Dead Man Jack, never look back.
(laughter)

COWBOY: (growling, snarling) Where did you hide my money? You no good, double-crossing, smelly old piece of vulture bait!

PROSPECTOR: (laughter) Who double-crossed who? (laughter)

COWBOY: You stole my money from my saddlebags, you thieving old bounty hunter.

PROSPECTOR: It wasn't your money, you smelly old bandit! The bounty on you wasn't near enough. I *earned* that money.

HARRY: (whispering) The Prospector is the bounty hunter, Silver Dollar Dan!

GILLIAN: (whispering) And the Cowboy is Dead Man Jack!

HARRY: (whispering) Shhhh. Listen.

DEAD MAN JACK/Cowboy: I've told you every year for 125 years—never steal from a thief!

SILVER DOLLAR DAN/Prospector: I've told you every year for 125 years—never double-cross a bounty hunter!

DEAD MAN JACK/Cowboy: Oh, but I got you good! When you fell asleep in the train car, taking me in to the sheriff...

SILVER DOLLAR DAN/Prospector: I don't need to hear your gloat.

DEAD MAN JACK/Cowboy: I took my WANTED POSTER and shaded my silver hair to make it look black like yours...

SILVER DOLLAR DAN/Prospector: You never tire of your own yappin' do you?

DEAD MAN JACK/Cowboy: Then I shaded in my silver hat to make it black like yours.

SILVER DOLLAR DAN/Prospector: You ain't gonna get my goat.

DEAD MAN JACK/Cowboy: It was a fine piece of work. You should have been there.

SILVER DOLLAR DAN/Prospector: I *was* there.

DEAD MAN JACK/Cowboy: You were asleep! Then I reached down and plucked one of the silver spokes off my spurs and used it for my missing tooth. So *you* were the only toothless one in the train car! You looked just like my WANTED POSTER!

SILVER DOLLAR DAN/Prospector: When the doors of the train swung open. You held up that poster and pointed at me. I didn't even get a chance to wipe the sleep out of my eyes before the sheriff threw a noose 'round my neck and strung me up.

DEAD MAN JACK/Cowboy: Yeah, the sheriff strung up the bounty hunter and let the thief go free!

SILVER DOLLAR DAN/Prospector: Oh, but I had the last laugh, didn't I?

DEAD MAN JACK/Cowboy: (snarling) You went prospecting in my saddlebags! Then hid my money so I can't find it! For 125 years I've been traipsing this trail looking for my money.

SILVER DOLLAR DAN/Prospector: (laughing) If you ever got the clue, I'd be amazed.

DEAD MAN JACK/Cowboy: But you didn't utter a

clue. You wasted your last snake's breath singing some lame brain song.

GILLIAN: Harry, that's it. The clue to finding the buried money is in the song.

HARRY: What are the words? I don't remember.

GILLIAN: I do. "I hid my silver on this lonesome trail. Three paces past the moon and a rusty nail."

HARRY: But what does that mean?

GILLIAN: Look! The moon is coming out from behind the storm clouds. It's shining a beam of light—where is it hitting?

HARRY: That tree. It's awfully close to the cliff...

SFX: FOOTSTEPS RUNNING

GILLIAN: Look! Somebody pounded a nail in this old tree!

HARRY: And the shadow from the nail is almost like a finger pointing to...

SFX: HORSE STOMPS, WHINNIES

GILLIAN: The Phantom, up on the bluff!

SFX: HOOVES POUNDING

HARRY: The very spot! The Phantom is pounding the dirt and uncovering...

SFX: CLINKING OF SILVER COINS

SILVER DOLLAR DAN/Prospector: You are the stupid one, aren't you?

DEAD MAN JACK/Cowboy: Why you four flushing, side winding...

SILVER DOLLAR DAN/Prospector: You egg sucker...

DEAD MAN JACK/Cowboy: I don't know why I put up with you all these years. I'm going to get my money if it's the last thing I do!

SILVER DOLLAR DAN/Prospector: Stay away from those silver coins!

DEAD MAN JACK/Cowboy: What do you mean?

SILVER DOLLAR DAN/ Prospector: You double-crossing outlaw!

DEAD MAN JACK/Cowboy: They're my silver coins!

SILVER DOLLAR DAN/Prospector: They're my silver coins!

DEAD MAN JACK/Cowboy: You old vulture bait, you!

ACT III, SCENE 4

SFX: HORSE GALLOPING

ARVIN: Whoa Bullet! Slow down Bullet! Help! Help! Runaway horse!! Somebody do something!!!

GILLIAN: It's Arvin! Pull on the reins!

HARRY: Arvin, try to jump off!

ARVIN: Get out of the way everybody! I can't stop!

GILLIAN: Arvin jump! Hurry! You're headed right toward the cliff!!!

HARRY: Get off, Arvin! Now!

ARVIN: AAAHH!!!

SFX: LASSO ROPE SPINNING

SMOKEY JOE: Hold on there Marvin, I've got you!

EBENEEZER: Smokey Joe gallops behind Arvin, spinning a lasso in the air. Just as Arvin gets close to the cliff and the Phantom Horse, the lasso drops around Arvin's shoulders.

As Smokey Joe pulls Arvin to safety, Bullet slides to a stop, pushing the silver coins over the side of the cliff into the cavern below.

SFX: CLINKING OF COINS FALLING ON ROCKS

GILLIAN: Oh no!

HARRY: Oh, all that money!

ARVIN: Oh!

DEAD MAN JACK/Cowboy: My money! It's at the bottom of the canyon!

SILVER DOLLAR DAN/Prospector: (laughter) After all these years. Who would've thought...

DEAD MAN JACK/Cowboy: Dadburn it! It was jest finding its way back into my saddlebags.

SILVER DOLLAR DAN/Prospector: It's a lowdown lizard's luck.

DEAD MAN JACK/Cowboy: My silver dollars are gone for good.

SILVER DOLLAR DAN/Prospector: Now you don't have to look for 'em no more.

DEAD MAN JACK/Cowboy: (accusing) So you think we're squared up now?

SILVER DOLLAR DAN/Prospector: I didn't say we were squared up.

DEAD MAN JACK/Cowboy: You're spoutin' off like we're squared up.

SFX: WIND

SILVER DOLLAR DAN/Prospector: (shift) Hey, that wind's blowin' in a different direction.

DEAD MAN JACK/Cowboy: You're right. It surely is.

SILVER DOLLAR DAN/Prospector: What d'ya make of that?

DEAD MAN JACK/Cowboy: I think it's time to move camp, Dan. What d'ya say?

SILVER DOLLAR DAN/Prospector: Yup. Looks like we're at the end of this trail, Jack. Phantom? Are you comin'?

SFX: HORSE WHINNIES

ACT III, SCENE 5

HARRY: Arvin, let me give you a hand.

GILLIAN: Arvin, are you okay?

ARVIN: Uh, yeah. Ah, Sure. (complimenting) Gillian, you actually figured out that clue, I'm amazed. I'm glad I didn't miss it.

GILLIAN: Thanks. (complimenting) And you weren't that bad riding Bullet. I thought you'd be worse.

ARVIN: Thanks.

SMOKEY JOE: Well, is everybody ready to head back to camp?

GILLIAN, HARRY & ARVIN: Yeah.

HARRY: That was a...a...

SMOKEY JOE: A little delay. We'll be back on the trail first thing in the morning. It's the same, authentic trail used by outlaws, desperadoes and cattle rustlers over 100 years ago. Yup, we'll start driving these ill-tempered, longhorn cattle through wild and desolate country.

There's coyotes and rattle snakes. There's the blistering sun, blinding dust storms, and wild rivers to cross. Then sometimes, just sometimes, there's a double-crossing, thieving cowboy riding right along beside you. And you don't know it until it's too late.

DEAD MAN JACK & SILVER DOLLAR DAN: (singing)
    I hid my silver on this lonesome trail.
    Three paces past the moon and a rusty nail.

But I got hung up with a noose.
I tried, but I couldn't get loose.
I never made it back.
Now they call me Dead Man Jack.

Dead Man Jack, never look back.
Dead Man Jack, never look back.

THE END

Stay tuned for scenes
from our
next episode of

CREEPERS Mysteries
Toadies

Movie for the Ear Trailer

Toadies

SFX: LOW RUMBLING of TOADS CROAKING, then the sound of BROOMS BRUSHING.

EBENEEZER: Have you ever been in a dark woods with just the trees and the toads? Have you ever been afraid of what a toadie can do in the dark? (STING) Get ready for this episode of Creepers Mysteries. Here it comes ...*Toadies.*

In the school hallway, Gillian is showing Arvin and Harry a piece of paper.

GILLIAN: This is my drawing of how to decorate the old Hamstead Farm for the Drama Club's Halloween Party.

ARVIN: (pointing) What's that thing?

GILLIAN: It's a prickly old vine we're going to wind up the staircase.

HARRY: Spooky...

Mr. Chad, the drama teacher, is directing the play for the Halloween party.

MR. CHAD: Now you all know the local legend of Hamstead Farm, which is where we'll be having our Halloween party. So, regardless of whether or not you believe the legend, it makes a great play for Halloween.

As the actors read through the play, the rest of you close your eyes. Pretend that you are at Hamstead Farm that very Halloween night in 1824.

SFX: WOLVES HOWLING, WIND HISSING, BRANCHES BEATING AGAINST WINDOWS, RATTLING DOORS ON HINGES.

MR. CHAD: (Narrating the play) It's not a safe night for man or beast....or witch. By the moon's glow, the witch's largest toadie hops along the dirt path toward the barn. A floating broom follows the toadie, sweeping away its tracks.

SFX: HOP, THUD, BRUSH

Harry and Arvin are gathering decorations in the woods behind Hamstead Farm.

HARRY: Look at this gnarled old oak tree. It's got a large, prickly vine around it—just like Gillian's drawing.

ARVIN: Yeah! Ugh! This vine is too thick.

HARRY: We need a knife.

ARVIN: Hey, did it just get dark really fast?

HARRY: Yeah, it did. We better hurry.

EBENEEZER: A toad hops on Arvin's shoe. He shakes his foot to get it off.

ARVIN: I have a feeling we're not alone.

EBENEEZER: Out of the darkness, a group of toads appear. They stare at Arvin with beady eyes. They don't move. They barely blink. Arvin freezes.

ARVIN: (scared) What's with all these toads all of a sudden?

EBENEEZER: The toads surround them both now, their beady eyes almost floating in the dark.

HARRY: (whispering) This is really weird. Let's get our decorations and get out of here.

SFX: HOWLING WIND, TOADS CROAKING

MUSIC: SUSPENSEFUL

EBENEEZER: The toads move toward Harry and Arvin, closer and closer.

Later, in the woods behind Hamstead Farm:

MUSIC: VINE UNWINDING

EBENEEZER: Slowly the vine releases its hold and peels away from the gnarled old tree. The yellow evil eye in the knothole blinks. Then a second eye appears. The bark begins to bubble and roll in small waves, forming the face of a woman—no, of a witch—pushing her way out.

EVIL WITCH: (howling in frustration) Removing the vine removed only part of the curse! (shift) But look, the woods are sprinkled with bright beady eyes and familiar shadows.

SFX: CROAKS

EVIL WITCH: I have summoned you, my loyal toadies, to break the curse which has held me prisoner in this tree for hundreds of years.

SFX: RUSTLING OF DEAD LEAVES

EVIL WITCH: First, I will drop three branches from this tree. When they hit the ground, small brooms they will be.

SFX: WHOOSH, DROP, MAGICAL STING

EVIL WITCH: Now, toadies, take these brooms. Use them as wands to ZAP three jealous souls. Put them in the tree to set me free. Put them in the tree instead of me.

——————————————

Back at the Hamstead Farmhouse, it's decorated for the Halloween party, and it's full of kids from the drama club.

SFX: (growing louder) HOP, THUD, BRUSH...

GILLIAN: Harry! What is that? I'm scared!

HARRY: It's coming from the back of the house.

ARVIN: You mean *they* are coming from the back of the house. Look!

SFX: CROWD SCREAMS, CROWD RUNS, DOOR SLAMS.

ARVIN: The crowd is running out the front door, and the toads are coming in the back!

HARRY: They're not like any toads I've ever seen.

GILLIAN: They're huge! Bigger than huge! They're humongous!!

SFX: HOP, THUD, BRUSH

GILLIAN: They're getting closer. DO SOMETHING!! Aaahh!!

Harry, Gillian and Arvin run out the front door, but they don't hear it slam. A floating broom holds it open while the toadies pass through.

HARRY: Run to the barn. Hurry!

SFX: HOP, THUD, BRUSH...

A toadie points the bristles of its suspended broom at one of the kids.

SFX: WHOOSH!

EBENEEZER: There's a flash of green light, then a gurgling sound, then silence. Someone has been vaporized into the broom. But who?

For more about
Creepers Mysteries—Book 2
Toadies

go to www.CreepersMysteries.com

Before You Go

Now that you've met Harry, Gillian and Arvin, let me tell you a few things about them that you don't know.

Gillian has a "thing" about the number 3. It's gotten her into a lot of trouble. No one knows why she's so hung up on that number, how it all started, or what's going to happen because of it. No one, that is, except Gillian.

Arvin thinks he knows just about everything. This can be mildly annoying for those around him, especially Gillian. But it becomes dangerous for Arvin when he tells the wrong people that he knows something, when he really doesn't. Very dangerous.

"Harry" isn't his real name, it's his nickname. People started calling him Harry because he turned up in so many hair-raising episodes of Creepers Mysteries. But there's more to it than that. He guards his real name with his life. Because if anyone found out—well, you don't want to know what would happen...

Or do you?

Maybe you'll find out more about Harry, Gillian and Arvin by reading upcoming episodes of Creepers Mysteries.

It's something I would do...

—Connie

www.creepersmysteries.com

About Ebeneezer Stump

Ebeneezer Stump appeared at my door one day without an appointment. He had a small black bag that he set on a chair. Out of the bag he pulled a lectern (which was much bigger than the bag, so I still don't know how he managed that).

He set up the lectern on...well, actually—nothing. It floated in the air. And so did he.

Next, Ebeneezer reached down and pulled out a large, heavy book.

The room grew darker and darker... Suddenly, two candles jumped out of the bag and hovered above the book. They sprinkled just enough light on the pages so Ebeneezer could read them.

I sat entranced as Ebeneezer began to speak, first revealing only tidbits and scribbled notes. Then I heard characters' voices, and more than one spooky sound.

Finally, he said, "If you're going to write Creepers Mysteries, Connie, you better get started. First, you've got to get into a creepy mood. Try turning the lights down low and crank the fun up high. Create Creepers

Mysteries in the dark, using only your imagination. When you're ready, use this flashlight and write down the lines."

Then he disappeared.

I've kept that flashlight by my side ever since.

Throughout the years, Ebeneezer has continued to appear and disappear at just the right times. He nudges, cajoles and inspires me as I write each Creepers Mystery.

The Creepers characters and I have all become very good friends. And we've all gotten to know the elusive Ebeneezer as well as anybody can...which is not very well at all.

But there's one thing we do know for sure: absolutely nothing creepy can happen without Ebeneezer Stump—and the right lighting.

—Connie Kingrey Anderson
Ebeneezer's Friend

About the Author

Connie Kingrey Anderson has a B.A. in Theatre from the University of Minnesota, and a Masters of Fine Arts in Drama from the University of Georgia. She lives on a colorful cul-de-sac in Minnesota with one funny husband, two furry friends, and three times the average imagination.

Whenever she's in the mood for something fun and entertaining, she jumps into another Creepers Mystery. She hopes you'll do the same...

Visit us online at
www.CreepersMysteries.com